# STEVEN MAC[...]

# MICRO-CONCERTO

## for Percussionist and Mixed Quintet

## Solo Percussion Part

HENDON MUSIC

DISTRIBUTED BY

7777 W. BLUEMOUND RD. P.O. BOX 13819 MILWAUKEE, WI 53213

www.boosey.com
www.halleonard.com

# NOTE BY THE COMPOSER

Several years ago I attended The Percussive Arts Society National Convention. There I witnessed a ninety-minute clinic on state of the art techniques for playing crash cymbals. I confess that there was something humorously esoteric about the event, but I left inspired to imagine particular ways to coax sound out of pieces of wood, metal and skin instead of simply hitting things. It also woke me to the fact that the first step in writing for percussion is to invent the instrument and a playing technique. Percussionists tend to have an adventurous attitude about this: if they can reach it with an arm or leg, or hold it in the mouth it is fair game. I'm fascinated by the one-man-band mentality of juggling contrasting timbres produced by a gamut ranging from finely crafted instruments to kitchen utensils, and hobby shop paraphernalia.

In addition to providing a virtuoso "vehicle" for the percussionist, *Micro-Concerto* also explores a variety of more complex roles that the individual can play in relation to the ensemble. In movement I: Chords and Fangled Drum Set, the rhythm is front and center. I imagine that the piano chords harmonize the rhythm instead of the rhythm measuring the harmonies.

Movement II: Interlude #1 Vibes Solo, is a short, lyrical ballad.

In Movement III: Click, Clak, Clank, the percussionist is neither an accompanying rhythm section nor leading melody. I think of it as a contextualizing and interpreting narration spoken in some imaginary tongue-clicking language.

In Movement IV: Interlude #2 Marimba and Cello, the two instruments are completely co-dependent; the story is told only by their interplay. In some sense they are a single instrument with timbres no more disparate than the clickers and samba whistle that are part of the percussionist's instrument in movement III. This movement flows without pause into movement V: Tune in Seven. In the first half of the movement the percussionist is one of six players tossing around a set of variations on the Tune. Toward the end the percussionist returns to the "fangled drum set" and shifts the focus back to what must be (along with singing) the most fundamental form of musical expression—hitting things in time.

The two interludes are played on big, standard pieces of percussion "furniture," but the main movements focus on small moves and subtle distinctions. They are full of fussy descriptions of how to play some hand-held "toy" just so. This micro-management of small muscle groups, and the fact that the concerto soloist is accompanied by the smallest orchestra imaginable, suggested the title.

—Steven Mackey, 1999

*Commissioned by a Meet the Composer grant for the New York*
*New Music Ensemble, the San Francisco Contemporary Music Players,*
*and the California E.A.R Unit.*

*First performed on November 3, 1999 New York, New York*
*Daniel Druckman, percussion / New York New Music Ensemble*

# INSTRUMENTATION

Flute (Alto Flute, Piccolo)
Clarinet in B♭ (Bass Clarinet)
Violin
Violoncello

## Percussion

[Vibraphone/Bass drum/low Tom-tom/med Tom-tom/
high Tom-tom/Almglocken/tuned Cowbell/2 Congas/
*Claves/sml high Triangle/Susp. cymbal/
pedal kick Bass drum/low Asian drum/low Samba whistle/clickers/
Bongos/2 Timbales/Woodblocks/2 piccolo woodblocks/sml Cowbell/
log drum/mounted Castanets/sm Guiro/Egg shaker/
mounted Tambourine/Jingles/Vibraslap/Sizzle cymbal/
Chinese cymbal/Crash cymbal/sml Chinese gong/
Cans/Bean pod rattle/Bottles]

(*hold Claves in hands (not in traditional way,
cradled in knuckles). Gently balance Claves
between thumb and middle finger. Ellipses
indicates that Claves ricochet in short "trill."
Clave in left hand should be inserted into
plane of Triangle (supported above Conga),
and be quite close (within an inch) of the
bottom side of Triangle to easily drop down
and strike Triangle after each Clave trill.)

Piano

Duration: 19 minutes

Performance materials are available from the Boosey & Hawkes Rental Library

Percussion

*written for Daniel Druckman and the New York New Music Ensemble*

# MICRO-CONCERTO

## Part 1: Chords and Fangled Drumset

Hold Claves in hands (not in traditional way - cradled in knuckles).
Gently balance Claves between thumb and middle finger.
Ellipses indicates that Claves ricochet in short "trill."
Clave in left hand should be inserted into plane of Triangle (supported above Conga),
and be quite close (within an inch) of the bottom side of Triangle
to easily drop down and strike Triangle after each Clave trill.

STEVEN MACKEY

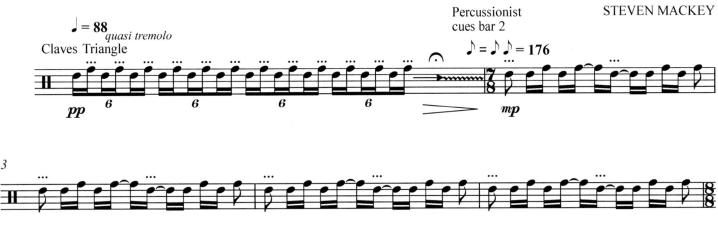

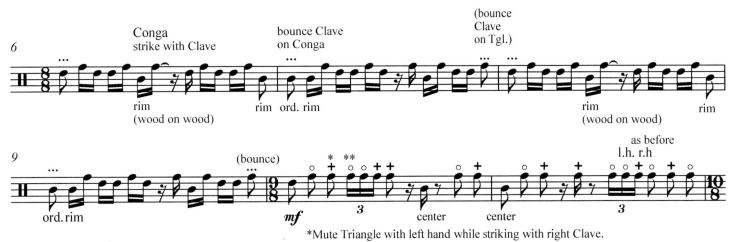

*Mute Triangle with left hand while striking with right Clave.

** With right Clave inside plane of Triangle, articulate 1st sixteenth of triplet:
by striking right side of Triangle with right Clave, 2nd sixteenth: bottom side
with right Clave, 3rd: 'clanking' Clave against left side of Triangle by grabbing
Triangle with left hand following eighth: strike bottom of Triangle with right
Clave while muting with left hand.

Allow left Clave to bounce on Conga near edge while drawing it to rim.
Sound starts as wood on Conga then "glissandos up" to wood on wood.

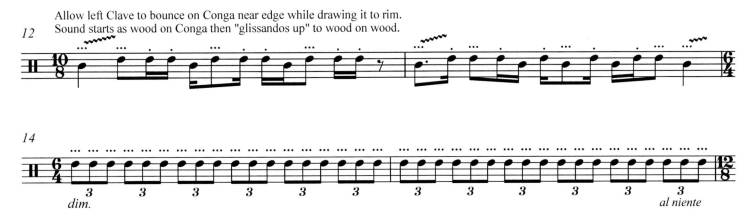

Percussion

**\*\*** as before, allow left clave to bounce on Conga near edge while drawing it to rim.
Sound starts as wood on Conga then "glissandos up" to wood on wood.

**\*** mute Triangle with l.h. while striking with r.h.
**\*\*** as before, l.h. r.h.

## Part 2: Interlude #1 - Vibes Solo

# Part 3: Click, Clak, Clank

In one hand hold small Guiro, in the other hold Clicker between thumb and index finger and small wooden mallet for scraping and striking. Samba Whistle in mouth.

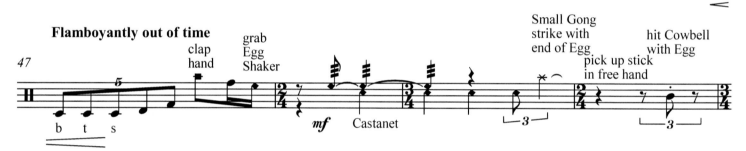

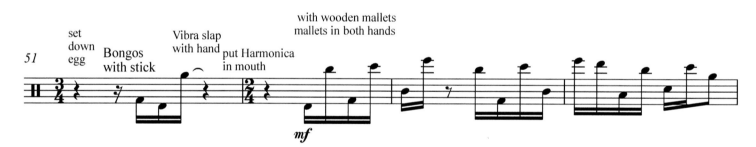

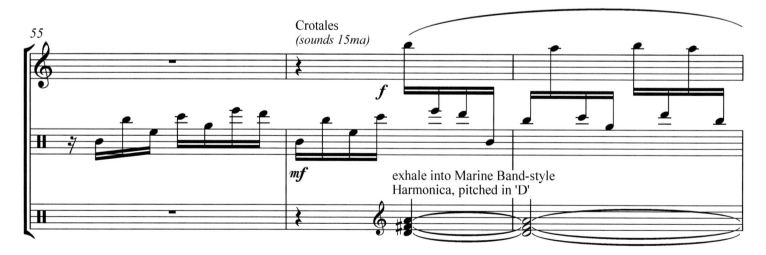

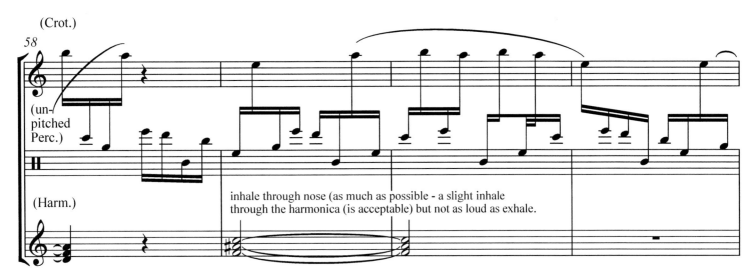

inhale through nose (as much as possible - a slight inhale
through the harmonica (is acceptable) but not as loud as exhale.

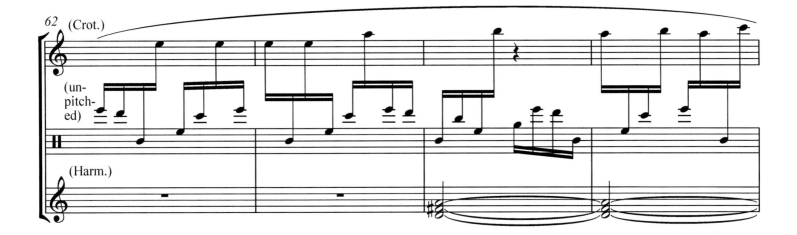

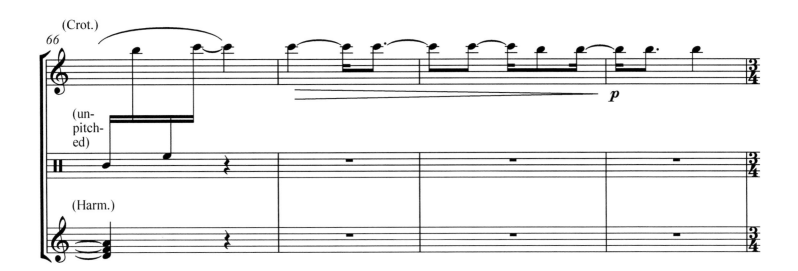

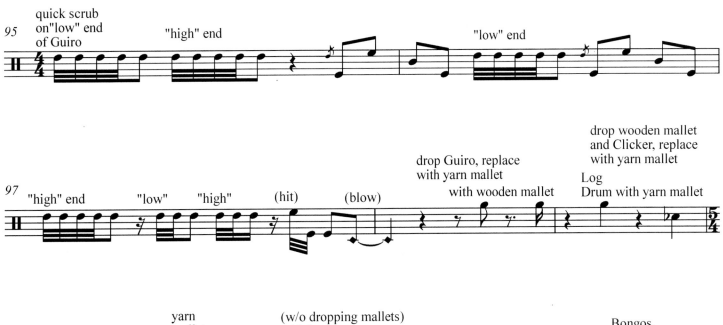

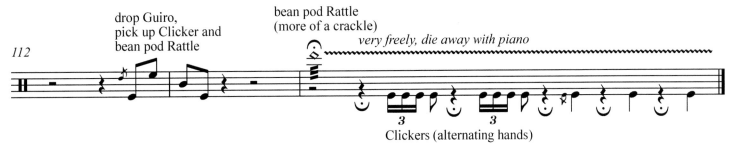

Pace so that last Clicker note is just before completely decay of Piano.
Do not synchronize last Clicker with Ped. release.

# Part 4: Interlude #2 - Marimba and Cello

♩ = 116-126 **Steady**

Graduated mallets:
hard - upper right hand; Med.- lower right hand
med. soft - upper left hand; soft - lower left hand

♩ = 126

*dim. poco a poco*

d.s.    **attacca**

## Part 5: Tune in Seven

(♩ = 126)

♩. = ♩ = 88      ♩ = ♩.

♩. = 88

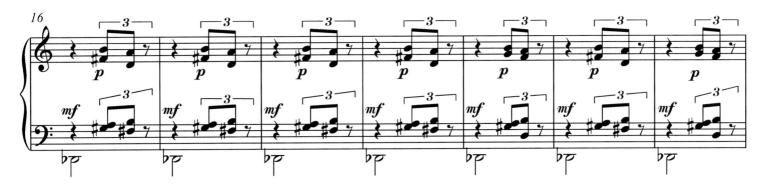

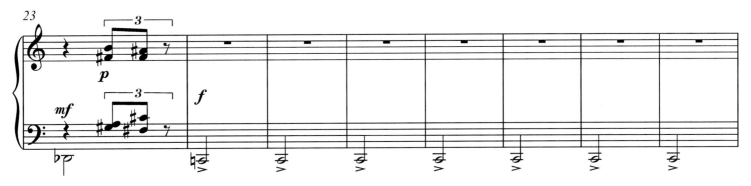

**47**

**52**

**55**

**58**

**61**

66

72

76

to non-pitched
perc. station #2

80
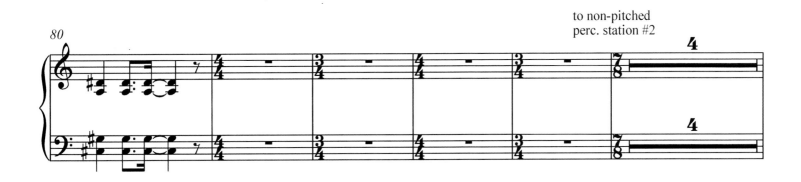

SOLO: sparse, stumbling,
herky-jerky, metrically confusing,
drum stick in one hand, yarn mallet
in other - ad lib unless indicated.

Use butt of
wooden handle
to press down on
skin & produce
pitch bend

bounce
mallet
handle
on rim

dead
stroke

**Perc. Station #2**

*starting to groove*

*starting to find groove*

(keep bass drum fairly quiet)

bounce
on rim

choked

**Although dead stroke on wood block may
not greatly effect sound, that mode of attack
is important to the character.

*exuberant*

Samba Whistle
in mouth

*freely, as if improvised
dramatic, recitativo*

123

choked

**fp**

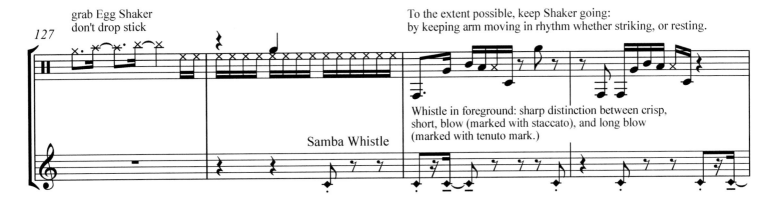

grab Egg Shaker
don't drop stick

127

To the extent possible, keep Shaker going:
by keeping arm moving in rhythm whether striking, or resting.

Samba Whistle

Whistle in foreground: sharp distinction between crisp,
short, blow (marked with staccato), and long blow
(marked with tenuto mark.)

hit anything and everything
except Cymbals

131

*frantic flurry*

*controlled 16ths*

hit anything and everything
except Cymbals

135

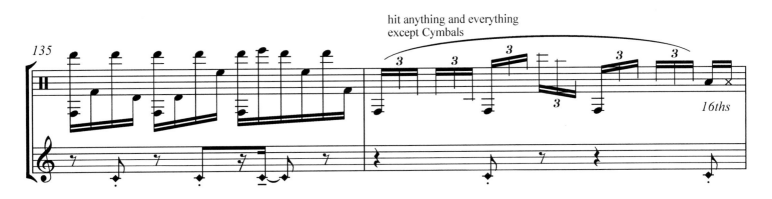

*16ths*

hit anything and everything (save Cymbal for downbeat)

to Perc. Station #1

137

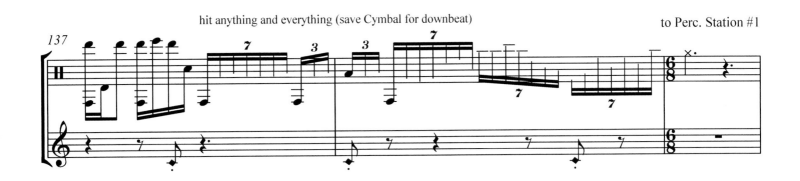

### Perc. Station #1
Claves & Triangle (as in Mvt. I)

140

144

147

150

153
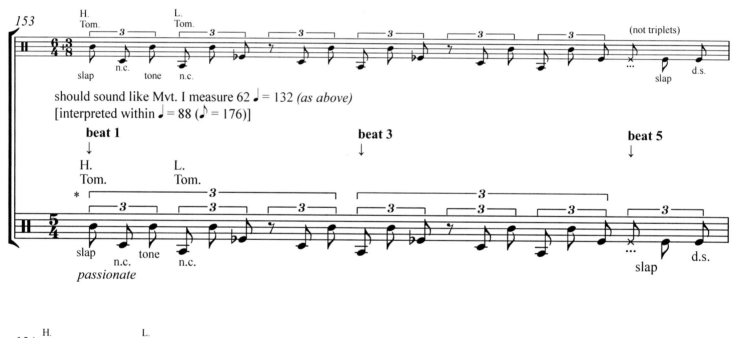

should sound like Mvt. I measure 62 ♩ = 132 *(as above)*
[interpreted within ♩ = 88 (♪ = 176)]

154
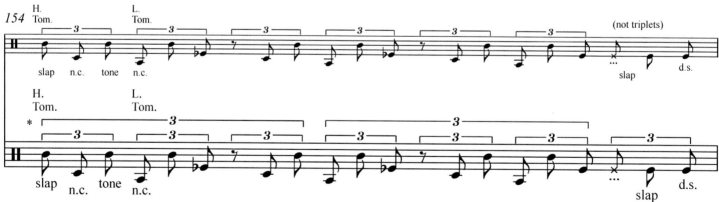

* It is most important that the percussion part is committed and has the feel it did in Mvt I. Synchronization with ensemble is less important, it should feel like like the 5/4 ensemble phrase, and the 6/4 + 3/8 (@ ♩ = 132) percussion phrase from the beginning, are the same length.

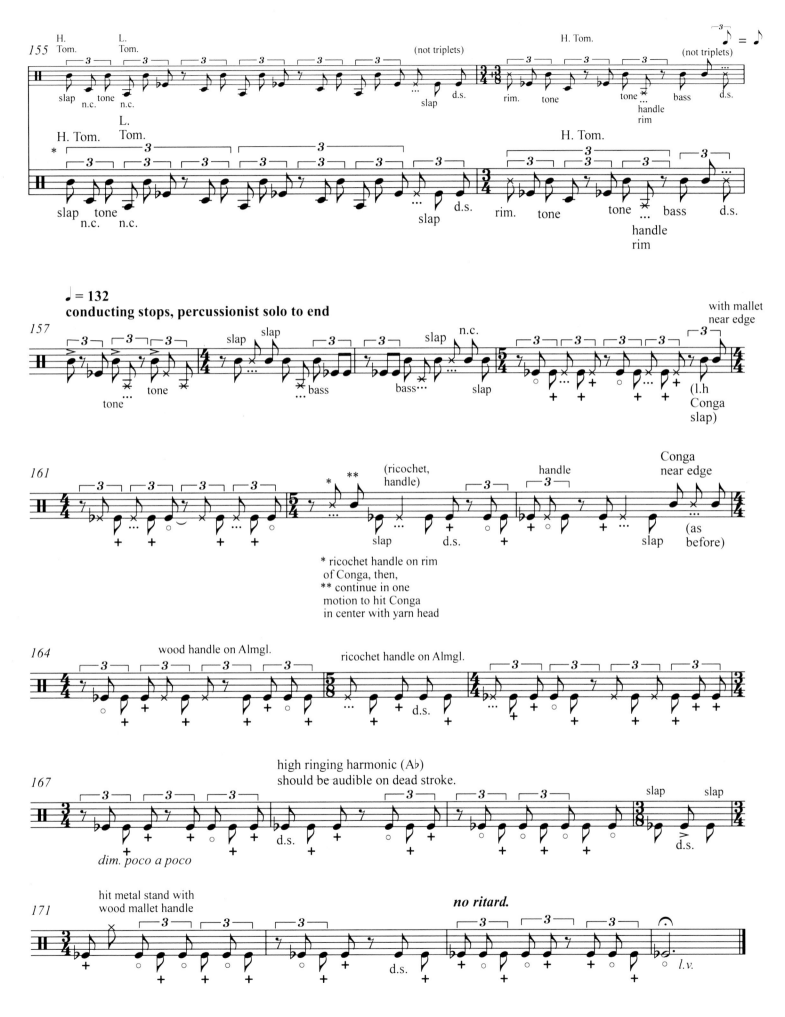